Success with

Climbing plants

ANGELIKA WEBER
KARIN GREINER

Series Editor:
LESLEY YOUNG

MEREHURST

Introduction

Contents

Say farewell to boring, bare walls on balconies and patios! By using graceful climbing plants and luxuriantly flowering trailing plants, any patio and even the smallest balcony can be transformed into an oasis of greenery. The special feature of climbing plants is that they grow vertically, thus saving on space and leaving plenty of room for a table, a recliner or a parasol.

In this guide, Angelika Weber and Karin Greiner provide a mass of information on the botany of these versatile plants and their requirements as to position and care all year round. Step-by-step illustrations in full colour provide comprehensive information about plant care, propagation and protection against damage by pests and diseases.

In the chapter on design, you will find imaginative ideas, specially created for this book by flower artist Martin Weimar, for growing plants together in pots, large containers and hanging baskets, including advice on creating flowering screens to give you added privacy and also to help to muffle the levels of outside noise. By following the advice supplied by these two experienced gardening authors, even readers who have little previous knowledge of gardening should find that their efforts are successful and relatively problem-free.

White-flowered Russian vine (Polygonum) on a patio.

Morning glory (Ipomoea) – a winding plant.

Bougainvillea has brilliant flowers.

The authors

Both Angelika Weber and Karin Greiner are botanists and biologists with a keen interest in ecology. Between them they have many years of experience in all areas of gardening and are authors of several reference works on gardens and plant care.

The authors wish to thank Thomas Hagen for his valuable advice and help with research during the writing of this book.

Plant arrangements

Martin Weimar is a gardener and flower arranger who has contributed to numerous flower design exhibitions. For many years he has run courses on artistic design using plants and is the author of several successful books on the subject of designing with plants. The specially commissioned plant arrangements shown in this book were created by Martin Weimar and photographed by Jürgen Stork.

NB: Please read the Authors' Notes on page 62 in order that your enjoyment of climbing and hanging plants may remain unspoiled.

Planned greenery

Climbing plants with exotic-looking shoots or tendrils and luxuriant hanging plants can create a very atmospheric effect on a balcony or patio. The important thing is to plan carefully and maintain a delicate touch when blending the colours of flowers and containers. The following pages will tell you all you need to know for the successful creation of a haven of colour and foliage.

Left: *Climbing plants enhance the corner of this patio.*
Above: *Clematis hybrid.*

Planned greenery

Three-dimensional gardening

Even if you have very little room, balconies and patios can be transformed into a green oasis – providing all dimensions of the available space are utilized effectively. Climbing plants and hanging plants provide many opportunities for innovative design. The growing of foliage on buildings and pergolas has a long tradition. Today, however, there are so many different species and varieties of climbing plants to choose from – from plain green ones like the ivies (*Hedera* species), right through to conspicuous flowering species like *Campsis* – that there is bound to be something to suit every taste. Even among hanging plants alone, the range of varieties is overwhelming. For example, all over Britain and Europe fuchsias, pelargoniums and petunias can be seen growing over balcony railings and in hanging baskets, pots and boxes.

Useful as well as decorative

Climbing plants on balconies and patios are not just visually pleasing. During the summer, the natural process by which they release moisture through evaporation (transpiration) increases humidity so that they create a desirable mini-climate as well as providing shade. Plants like the *Aristolochia* species form a dense curtain of leaves and will even give some protection against noise. Foliage-covered walls also serve to create a better climate within a house: green plants growing on a south-facing wall provide shade in summer and thereby combat the build-up of heat during the day. During the winter, when the plants have lost their foliage, the sun is able to warm up the walls again. On the other hand, climbing plants growing on the north-facing wall of a house will help to prevent loss of heat through the walls – a particularly desirable effect in the winter.

A small balcony, large patio or terrace

The way you design and plan your patio or balcony refuge will depend a great deal on the available space. A small balcony means that you will have to make do with hanging plants in balcony boxes and a few pots containing climbing plants. A generously proportioned patio will, of course, offer more extensive possibilities for planning. Both balconies and patios have one thing in common, they are always bounded by at least one wall which, in many cases, lends itself beautifully to being covered with greenery.

Our tip: The sides of balconies and patios can be provided with screens and windbreaks in the form of climbing plants in large containers (see p. 21).
NB: It goes without saying that climbing and hanging plants need to be set in positions that will meet their requirements. Sun-lovers should not be placed in the shade, while, conversely, shade-loving plants will not thrive in too much sun (see p. 12).

Short- or long-term planting

There is a huge range of climbing and hanging plants. Whether you prefer conspicuous, colourful flowers or the quieter shades of green plants, it is entirely a matter of individual taste what you choose. Permanent and easy-to-care-for groupings of plants can be created with perennial plants. Annuals will require more work but also allow you to enjoy a completely new design scheme every year.

Our tip: The best system is a combination of perennial and annual plants. The tables on pages 10-11 will give you an idea of many suitable species.

A lovely combination of ivy and a climbing rose. (Design p. 34.)

Botany

How plots climb
How plants climb

Many plants that climb
and wind originate from
tropical rainforests
where they evolved vari-
ous special techniques
in order to reach up
towards the light in the
dense, dark jungle. A
distinction can be made
between:
● plants that wind;
● plants with tendrils;
● plants with rooting
  suckers;
● ramblers.

1 Winding plants
a Right-winding plant.
b Left-winding plant.

shoots contrary to their
natural direction of
growth as this will
cause them to wither.

Plants that wind
(see illustration 1)

Plants that wind twist
the whole length of their
shoots around a sup-
port. Most species wind
to the left, or anti-clock-
wise. Among these are
the runner bean
(*Phaseolus coccineus*),
morning glory (*Ipomoea*
spp) and wisteria
(*Wisteria* spp). Right-
winding (clockwise)
species include hops
(*Humulus lupulus*) and
honeysuckle (*Lonicera*
spp). Make sure that
you do not tie up

Tendril-forming plants
(see illustration 2)

Parts of plants which
curl around supports
are called tendrils.
In the case of *leaf-ten-
dril plants* (see illustration 2a) like the sweet
pea (*Lathyrus odoratus*)
the tips of the leaves
have evolved into thin
tendrils which wind
around the support.
Leaf stem tendrils (see
illustration 2b), as found
in *Clematis* hybrids or
nasturtium (*Tropaeolum*
spp), are tendrils which
have formed from the
stem of the leaf and will
wind around the

branches of other
woody plants. There are
also several intermedi-
ate types.

Our tip: As tendril-form-
ing plants like to wind
around vertical sup-
ports, any support pro-
vided should have more
vertical than horizontal
arms. The individual
struts should not be too
thick otherwise very fine
tendrils will not be able
to wrap themselves
around them.

2 Plants with tendrils
a A leaf tip adapted to become a tendril gives the plants grip.
b The leaf stalk is adapted to become a tendril for climbing.

Ramblers

(see illustration 5)

Ramblers are plants which form prickles (like *Bougainvillea*), thorns (like blackberries and climbing roses) or barbed lateral shoots with which they are able to hold on to a support. You should also always tie some of the shoots to a supporting structure, as this will help the plant to climb.

Hanging plants

These do not constitute a separate botanical group. The term simply covers all plants which have long, flexible shoots that do not climb but hang down. Such plants are particularly suitable for hanging containers, balcony boxes or large, tall containers. Examples can be found on page 11. Hanging plants can also be encouraged to grow upwards by tying them to a support.

3 Climbing plant with suckers
Some climbers have evolved little sucker pads.

4 Climbing plant with rooting suckers
These plants climb by means of tiny adapted roots.

Plants with suckers

(see illustration 3)

Plants which produce suckers, like the wild vine (*Parthenocissus* spp) or *Vitis vinifera*, use adapted shoots to wind around a support. There are, however, some species of wild vine (e.g. *Parthenocissus tricuspidata, P. quinquefolia*) which form small adhesive pads or suckers. With the help of these suckers, the plants are able to cling to walls and may attain great heights.

Plants with rooting suckers

(see illustration 4)

These plants are also in a position to "climb" trees without any other support. Rooting suckers form along their shoots, which enable them to hold on to the support. Such plants include ivy (*Hedera* spp), the climbing hortensia (*Hydrangea anomala petiolaris*) and *Campsis* spp.

Our tip: Never allow plants with rooting suckers to climb up walls with defective rendering. They will penetrate the cracks and may damage the masonry (see p. 18).

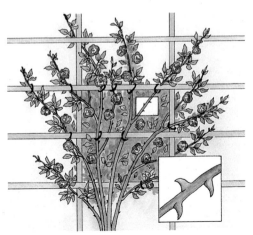

5 Rambling plants
These plants provide their own grip by means of thorns, prickles or barb-like lateral shoots.

Perennial climbing plants

Name	Flowering time Colour	Position	Height in m/ft	Method of climbing	Propagation	Comments
Actinidia spp/varieties kiwi fruit	lsp-msm white/yellow	○ ◐	3-8 m/10-26 ft	winding	seeds, cuttings	Two sexes; to obtain fruit plant out male and female specimens.
Campsis spp/varieties morning glory	msm-ea orange	○	4-10 m/13-33 ft	rooting suckers	cuttings, anchored shoots, grafting	Luxuriant flowers in warm positions, exotic flowers.
Clematis spp/hybrids	lsp-ma various	○ ◐	2-10 m/6-33 ft	tendrils	cuttings, grafting	Wide range of species and varieties; hybrids need shaded roots.
Euonymus fortunei and varieties	lsp-msm greenish	○ ●	3-5 m/10-16 ft	rooting suckers	cuttings	Evergreen; varieties with attractively coloured leaves.
Fallopia aubertii	msm-ma white	○ ●	8-15 m/26-49 ft	winding	cuttings, shoots	Grows bushy; masses of flowers.
Hedera spp/varieties ivy	ea-ma greenish-yellow	◐ ●	5-25 m/16-82 ft	rooting suckers	seed, cuttings	Evergreen; always undemanding.
Humulus lupulus hop	msm-lsm greenish	○ ◐	4-6 m/13-20 ft	winding	rhizomes	Provides visual, wind and noise screen; two sexes.
Hydrangea anomala petiolaris, climbing hortensia	esm-msm white	◐ ●	5-10 m/16-33 ft	rooting suckers	cuttings, anchored shoots	Attractive flower umbels; attractive autumn colouring.
Jasminum nudiflorum winter jasmine	lw-msp yellow	○ ◐	2-4 m/7-13 ft	rambling	cuttings, shoots	In mild winters, flowers from ew.
Lonicera spp honeysuckle	lsp-msm yellow red	◐	2-6 m/7-20 ft	winding	seed, cuttings	Pretty, scented flowers; fast growing.
Parthenocissus spp/ varieties, wild vine	esm-lsm yellow green	○ ◐	8-15 m/26-49 ft	tendrils	shoots, grafting	Beautiful autumn colouring; five-leafed vine will require support to begin with.
Pyracantha spp/varieties	esm-msm creamy white	○ ◐	3-5 m/10-16 ft	rambling	seed, cuttings	Conspicuous fruits, orange to red; undemanding.
Rosa spp/varieties climbing roses	lsp-ma various	○	2-5 m/7-16 ft	rambling	grafting	Demanding; many double and single varieties.
Rubus henryi bramble	esm-msm light pink	◐ ●	2-4 m/7-13 ft	rambling	cuttings, shoots	Evergreen; various leaf shapes.
Vitis spp grape vine	esm-msm yellow green	○ ◐	3-12 m/10-39 ft	tendrils	seed, cuttings, grafting	Wild varieties are undemanding; *Vitis vinifera* (grapevine) for warm positions.
Wisteria spp/varieties blue laburnum or wisteria	msp-esm blue, white	○ ◐	6-12 m/20-39 ft	winding	grafting	Pretty racemes; requires firm support.

Annual climbing plants

Name	Flowering time Colour	Position	Height in m/ft	Method of climbing	Growing method	Comments
Asarina spp/varieties	esm-ma various	○	2-3 m/7-10 ft	tendrils	seedlings under glass, plant out from lsp	Tie up young plants after they have been pricked out.
Cobaea scandens cathedral bell	msm-ma blue/violet, white	○ ◐	3-5 m/10-16 ft	tendrils	seedlings under glass, plant out from lsp	Conspicuous flowers; visual and wind screen; overwinter indoors.
Cucurbita pepo var. ovifera ornamental gourds	msm-ea yellow	○	3-5 m/10-16 ft	tendrils	directly sown in lsp or pre-sown in boxes	Striking fruits in many shapes and colours; fast growing.
Eccremocarpus scaber and varieties, Chilean glory	esm-ma various	○	3-4 m/10-13 ft	tendrils	seedlings under glass, plant out from lsp	Rapid growth; requires a sheltered position.

esp	early spring	esm	early summer	ea	early autumn	ew	early winter
msp	mid-spring	msm	mid-summer	ma	mid-autumn	mw	mid-winter
lsp	late spring	lsm	late summer	la	late-autumn	lw	late winter

Name	Flowering time Colour	Position	Height in m/ft	Method of climbing	Growing method	Comments
Humulus japonicus Japanese hop	msm-ea yellow green	◯ ●	4-5 m/13-16 ft	winding	Sow directly in lsp or pre-sow.	Fast growing; "Variegatus" is a variety with white/coloured foliage.
Ipomoea tricolor and varieties, morning glory ☠	msm-ma various	◯	1-3 m/3-10 ft	winding	Seedlings under glass, plant out from lsp.	Pretty flowers; plants need a sheltered spot.
Lathyrus odoratus and varieties, sweet pea ☠	esm-ea various	◯	1-3 m/3-10 ft	tendrils	Direct sowing in msp or pre-sow.	Pretty flowers; good for growing on fences; remove dead flowers.
Pharbitis spp/varieties ☠	esm-ea various	◯	2-3 m/7-10 ft	winding	Direct sowing in lsp or pre-sow.	No demands on soil, fertilize sparingly.
Phaseolus coccineus varieties, runner bean	esm-ea red, white	◯ ◑	3-4 m/10-13 ft	winding	Direct sowing from lsp.	Undemanding, robust; beans can be eaten after cooked; good visual screen.
Quamoclit spp ☠	msm-ma various	◯	2-3 m/7-10 ft	winding	Seedlings under glass, plant out from lsp.	*Quamoclit coccinea* can be sown out directly in lsp.
Rhodochiton atrosanguineus	msm-ma reddish-pink	◯	2-5 m/7-16 ft	tendrils	Seedlings under glass, takes a long time.	Novelty on the market which is also very attractive in hanging baskets.
Thunbergia alata, varieties black-eyed Susan	esm-ma various	◯	1-2 m/3-7 ft	winding	Seedlings under glass, plant out from lsp.	Flowers with black centres; needs a sheltered spot.
Tropaeolum peregrinum canary creeper	msm-ma yellow	◯ ◑	1-3 m/3-10 ft	tendrils	Seedlings under glass, plant out from lsp.	Good climber; also climbing *Tropaeolum* hybrids (*majus* varieties).

Hanging plants

Name	Flowering time Colour	Position	Care	Propagation	Comments
Begonia hybrids, tuber begonias	lsp-ma various	◯ ◑	Plenty of watering, fertilizing.	Divide tubers.	Large tubers can be overwintered in a frost-free position.
Brachycome iberidifolia blue daisy	msm-ea blue violet	◯	Water well, fertilize, remove deadheads immed.	Seedlings under glass, plant out from lsp.	Pretty as an underplanting for standards.
Campanula poscharskyana bellflower	lsp-ea blue	◯ ◑	Undemanding; do not over-water.	Division, cuttings, seed.	Shoots grow to 60 cm/24 in; over-winter in bright, frost-free position.
Convolvulus sabatius	lsp-ma blue	◯	Water well, fertilize.	Seedlings under glass, cuttings.	Overwinter plant in bright, frost-free position; flowers close in the evening.
Dianthus caryophyllus carnation	lsp-ea red	◯	Water well, fertilize.	Cuttings, sowing takes a long time.	High UV light required for plenty of flowers (good near mountains).
Erigeron karvinskianus	lsp-ea white pink	◯	Water and fertilize sparingly.	Seedlings under glass.	Plants can be overwintered in bright, just about frost-free position.
Fuchsia hybrids	esm-ma various	◯ ◑	Water well, fertilize, cut back often.	Cuttings	Position generally semi-shady; some fuchsias can stand direct sunlight.
Lotus berthelotii	esp-msp red	◯	Water well, fertilize, no water-logging.	Cuttings	Avoid dryness; overwinter plant in bright, frost-free position.
Pelargonium peltatum hybrids ☠	msp-ma various	◯	Water well, fertilize, no water-logging.	Cuttings, F-hybrids also sown out.	Overwinter plant in bright, frost-free position; some plants are self-tidying.
Petunia hybrids (*Pendula* group), petunia	lsp-ea various	◯	Water well, fertilize, remove deadheads immed.	Seedlings under glass.	A new group of varieties, Surfinia, flowers and grows luxuriantly.
Plectranthus coleoides	lsm-ea white	◯ ◑	Water sparingly, fertilize, easy to care for.	Cuttings	Overwinter the plant in a bright place; "Marginatus" has white edges.
Scaevola salgina	msp-ea blue	◯	Water well, fertilize, no waterlogging.	Difficult!	Pretty novelty with long shoots; very sensitive to chalk.

Planned greenery

The importance of the right position

Before going out to purchase hanging or climbing plants, you should take a good look at your balcony or patio. The light and climatic requirements of different species can vary a great deal, and these factors must be considered if you want to enjoy your plants for as long as possible. This is particularly important for perennial plants which are planted in the soil and trained against a house wall with the help of a permanently fixed climbing frame. Choosing is an easier matter in the case of plants which are grown in pots or large containers. If you realize that a certain plant is not doing well in a particular position, it is an easy matter to move it to another, more suitable one. The same goes for hanging plants.

Sun or shade

The decisive factor when choosing plants is the amount of light that will be available. Many climbing plants, such as *Clematis* hybrids or *Lonicera* species, feel most comfortable in bright but not constantly sunny positions. The natural habitats of these species are generally woodland clearings and along the edges of woods. This corresponds to a site on an east- or west-facing balcony or patio.

The prime requirement for the well-being of other plants may be warmth. They will do best in a sheltered spot with plenty of sunshine. Plants in this category generally originate from warm regions, like wisteria (*Wisteria sinensis*) from China, or *Campsis radicans* which comes from the southern USA. When placed on balconies or patios, they much enjoy the protective warmth reflected by white walls in south-facing positions.

Finally, there are a number of species which prefer a position with high humidity. Among these are the climbing hortensia (*Hydrangea anomala petiolaris*) or ivy (*Hedera* spp). They do best in semi-shady to shady positions, which means they will also thrive in north-facing positions.

For all of the above reasons, before purchasing it is a good idea to seek out as much information as possible about the particular requirements of light and position of any plant that appeals to you.

Head in the sun, feet in the shade

Climbing plants generally grow upwards very rapidly and are, therefore, able to send their shoots into the areas they prefer. However, many light-hungry plants, like *Clematis* hybrids or *Campsis* species, also definitely require shaded "feet". The rea-son for this is connected with the problem encountered by these species of not being able to transport enough water right to the tips of their very long shoots in full, bright sunlight. This does not mean that the entire plant has to be positioned in the shade. These species can also be planted in sunny positions and then surrounded with tall-growing or low-growing, but dense, bushy shrubs or summer flowers. The lower plants will provide the necessary shade. On the other hand, very rapidly growing plants should not be used in such an underplanting as they might draw too much water from the soil. One good example of underplanting for *Clematis* would be the evergreen lesser periwinkle (*Vinca minor*).

Our tip: It is possible to obtain clematis collars in the gardening trade, which are placed around the foot of the plant to provide the necessary shade.

Rhodochiton atrosanguineus is enchanting as a climber or a hanging plant.

Planned greenery

Summer foliage or ever-green?

Another important consideration when choosing plants is whether you prefer colourful foliage in the autumn or whether you would rather be surrounded with green throughout the cold season. Wild vine (*Parthenocissus* spp) produces the most wonderful shades of coloured leaves in the autumn, while ivy (*Hedera* spp) retains its leaves during the winter. The choice as to whether to have summer-green or evergreen plants as cover on a wall will play an important part in the regulation of the mini-climate on your balcony or patio. It has been proved that houses with green façades possess a much more balanced mini-climate. The green "cloak" not only reduces the effect of heavy rainfall and exposure to strong sunlight, it also filters dust and exhaust fumes and even cuts down on noise. In the case of evergreen plants, the cushion of air underneath the planting prevents rapid cooling down during the winter.

Annual climbing plants enable a particularly flexible design. Using these plants, you can decide anew each year how and with what colours you are going to decorate your balcony or patio. The tables on pages 10-11 give details of some of the available range of plants.

A green curtain in your living room

While wishing to have more greenery around their home, many people prefer it to be at a distance. Espaliers with a dense growth of leaves will occasionally encourage spiders and other insects to invade a living room or even a bedroom. On the other hand, many of these visitors are useful insects which keep pests like mosquitos and flies in check. Even if an occasional spider does make itself at home in a corner of your house, a fly screen can help to prevent the problem. If the "green curtain" on a patio or balcony is large and dense enough, birds may even nest in it and bring up their young. Some plants also provide winter food for birds.

Tips on buying plants

Plants are offered for sale in various ways.

Annuals can be obtained in the spring. The seeds are sown and propagated very early in nurseries and have often attained a good size and many lateral shoots capable of producing flowers by the time they are taken outside in the last month of spring. The best specimens command a high price.

Perennials can be obtained in three forms:

● Container plants are grown in pots and also sold in them. They should be completely free of weeds and have spread their roots well throughout the pot. The roots should not fill the pot entirely, however, nor be poking out of the drainage hole. Container plants are the most expensive ones to buy but should continue to grow well.

● Plants sold with their root-stocks are cheaper. The root-stock will be wrapped in hessian or jute sacking. When replanting, merely loosen the binding, without removing the fabric, as this will gradually rot away by itself.

● Plants with loose root systems are cheapest, but planting them involves a little more work. They should be watered beforehand and the roots should be cut back.

In principle, plants are more expensive depending on how large and mature they are, as this, in turn, means they have been replanted several times in nurseries and garden centres. If you want to accumulate greenery on your balcony or patio at a low cost, you can, of course, grow your own climbing and hanging plants from seed. This will take longer but is a most rewarding and enjoyable leisure occupation.

Flowering climbers on a free-standing screen and in the shape of a pillar.

Tips on growing your own plants can be found on pages 52-53.

Our tip: Supermarkets often sell plants at extremely good prices, but their quality is not usually top class. Mostly, you cannot assess this at a glance. Long-lived, expensive woody plants are best bought in garden centres or top class nurseries where the plants have been propagated. In addi-tion to receiving expert advice, you will also be able to choose from a much larger selection and can also consult the specialist staff at the garden centre or nursery later on if you encounter problems.

Scaevola saligna.

Planting in containers

Choosing containers

You will find plant containers in all shapes and sizes for balconies and patios: pots made of clay or ceramic, glazed or unglazed, boxes, troughs and urns made out of wood, concrete, plastic or stone, bowls and hanging containers.
● Choose the material and shape to suit the total composition (see the section on design).
● The containers should be large enough for the plants to have enough space to develop properly.

● Containers which are intended to be hung up should not be too heavy.
● Make sure that the containers possess drainage holes.
● Always choose frost-proof containers for plants that have to withstand cold winter conditions.

1 Climbing and hanging plants in a large container
Plant the climber with a support. Place the hanging plant on a slant beneath it.

Planting in boxes

Plants need plenty of room to grow. A box should always be at least 15 cm (6 in) wide and 20 cm (8 in) deep. The following basic rules apply:
● Make sure there are drainage holes.
● Insert a 5-cm (2 in) thick drainage layer of Hortag or gravel in the bottom.
● Lay a piece of interfacing fabric on the drainage layer to prevent the compost from being washed away.
● Put in some compost, insert the plant, fill the container with compost and press it down.
● Water carefully.
● If the box is to be hung up, make sure it is securely fixed (see p. 18).

Planting in a large container
(see illustration 1)

When planting climbing or hanging plants in a large container:
● The drainage hole should be covered with large pieces of broken pot.
● Insert a 5-cm (2 in)

thick drainage layer of Hortag or gravel.
● Fill the pot with 5-10 cm (2-4 in) of compost.
● Insert the climbing plant and its support in the pot and arrange the plant on the support.
● Place the hanging plant slightly at a slant in the pot.
● Fill out the spaces with compost, press it down and water well.

Hanging baskets
(see illustration 2)

Wire baskets filled with hanging plants are very attractive.
● Line the basket with large wads of water-retaining sphagnum moss (see illustration 2a).
● Cut out a round piece of polythene sheet and lay it in the basket; the piece should overlap the edge of the basket by about 10 cm (4 in). Cut holes or cross-shaped slits in the sheet, through which the plants will be inserted (see illustration 2b).
● Fill the basket with plant compost to just below the edge (see illustration 2c).

a   b

2 Planting in baskets *a Line a basket with moss.*
b Insert polythene sheeting and cut out holes.

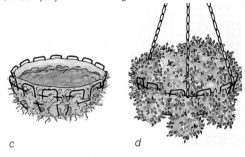

c   d

c Fill the basket with compost to just below the
edge. d Insert the plants, water well and hang up.

● First, insert the side plants from the outside through the layer of moss and sheeting, then press the compost down firmly around the roots. Overlapping sheeting should be folded over. Finally, plant the plants at the top of the basket.
● Carefully water the plants.
● Affix a means of hanging up the basket (see illustration 2d).
NB: If you wish to avoid using sphagnum moss in order to protect the environment, you can substitute soft interfacing fabric mats 3-5 cm (1-2 in) thick, wood shavings, coconut fibre or moss from your garden.

Planting in hanging containers

The plant container should not be too heavy and should be equipped with a stable means of hanging it up.
● Make sure there are drainage holes.
● Insert a drainage layer.
● Fill the container with compost and insert the plant.
● Water or briefly immerse the container in water.
● Make sure the container is hung from a stable fixture.

Climbing plants on a house wall
(see illustration 3)

The soil should be well prepared before planting as it tends to be rather dense along a wall. Annual climbing plants are best brought on as seedlings rather than sown directly into the soil. This will make them flower earlier. Woody plants, like *Clematis* hybrids or wild vine (*Parthenocissus* spp), should be planted in the autumn or early spring.

● If you are planting annuals, dig over the soil to a depth of 30 cm (12 in) and loosen it. Perennials need at least 50 cm (20 in) depth.
● Improve clay-rich soil with sand, sandy soil with compost and loosen thoroughly.
● Cover up the damp course insulation material along the house wall with polythene pond-lining material so that no damp can penetrate.
● Lean the plant towards the support.
● Fill the hole with soil and water well.
● Cover the soil with well-matured garden compost or bark mulch.

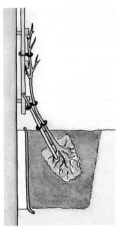

3 Climbers *should be planted at an angle and tied to a support.*

Planned greenery

Fixing containers securely

Make sure that you secure your plant containers properly so that you will have no worries about the safety of hanging baskets and boxes.

Hanging baskets should be hung high enough so that you do not need to stoop every time you pass underneath them. At the same time, they still need to be easily accessible for watering and other care.

The fixture should not only look attractive but also cope with the weight of the basket when filled with soil and plants. Also remember that, occasionally, rainwater may cause waterlogging.

A spot sheltered from the wind is preferable so that a storm or high wind cannot tear the basket from its anchorage.

There are various different fixtures for *balcony boxes*. Generally, they are clamped on to the balcony railing with adjustable fixtures, but they can also be attached to the wall by means of battens and screws. Wooden boxes are easily fixed directly to a wooden railing or barrier with L-shaped angle irons or clamps.

Our tip: If you have large, heavy balcony boxes, we suggest that you buy very heavy, strong metal fixtures that have been specially made to measure by a blacksmith and have them professionally installed.

How to fix hanging baskets and boxes securely

A hanging basket

Hanging containers require extremely secure fixtures, e.g. chains, wire or plastic rope. Rope made of natural fibres is easily frayed by rubbing against metal parts and may also rot in the damp. If the container is suspended from a wall or ceiling, always make sure the hook is very securely fixed. All wall fixtures should be provided with extra support from below.

Balcony boxes

● Find out the carrying capacity of both the railing and the balcony before installing heavy boxes.

● Adjust the width of the balcony box fixture to the thickness of the railing and screw it on tightly.

● Insert the boxes and clamp them on tightly from below with screws. The protruding lip will prevent tipping.

● Carefully water the plants and fix a water-catching device to the box so that the water cannot run away on to a neighbouring balcony or to the pavement below.

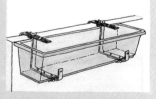

● From time to time, check the screws that hold the box or the hanging container, e.g. when watering.

● If you are spraying with plant protection agents, remove the hanging baskets and boxes so that your neighbours will not be affected.

Avoiding damage

As attractive as climbing plants are, if they are installed in a casual way, their natural tendency to grow quickly may also cause damage. Ivy, in particular, is notorious for this. Indeed, its suckers are known to penetrate gaps and cracks in old rendering and cracked masonry.

● Self-climbing plants should only be allowed to grow on undamaged walls. There should be no problems with mineral-based rendering, but care is advised with plastic-based rendering or plasterwork.

● It is better to avoid letting climbing plants grow on the walls of timbered buildings as the plants will tend to penetrate cracks in the wood. In addition, the increased humidity that will exist will attract the spores of various fungi.

● Species which produce very strong shoots, like *Wisteria* spp or *Campsis* spp, should be kept well away from gutters as they may dislodge them.

● If climbing plants are allowed to climb across a roof, their dead leaves may block the gutters. If the plants are encouraged to make use of proper climbing aids, like trellises and espaliers, no problems should occur.

Profuse flowers – Brachycome iberidifolia.

Your legal responsibility

Tenants who wish to grow plants on their balconies or patios should consider several factors. Usually, any alterations which affect the outer appearance of a house or apartment should be checked first with the landlord. The same goes for balcony boxes that you wish to install on the façade of the building. If you are intending to make extensive alterations, including the fixing of trellises or espaliers, or to grow self-climbing plants, you should definitely obtain permission from the owner of the building. When planting, give a little thought to your neighbours. Your plants should be held in check so that your neighbours are not hampered or hindered by them nor have to suffer from lack of light. The best plan is to discuss it with them first.

Climbing aids

The right support

(see illustration 2)

The kind of support required by a particular plant will depend on its individual method of climbing.

Plants with tendrils require lattice-shaped climbing aids, various types of which can be obtained in the gardening trade. Metal lattices, as used for reinforcement in the building profession, are ideal. They can be fixed to the wall with clamps (see illustration 2a).

Winding plants require vertical supports.

● Annuals will make do with gardening twine which is simply tied around a few hooks or nails. Knots in the string will provide additional purchase.

● Longer-living species wil require more stable structures as these will have to support increasing weight over a period of time. Secure wire rope to wall hooks fixed firmly to the wall (see illustration 2b).

Rambling plants require predominantly horizontal support. This may take the form of a structure made out of wooden battens (see illustration 2c) or may be lattices as used for winders. The distance between the battens

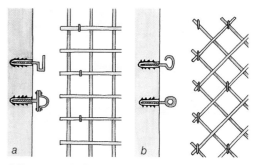

2 Permanently fixed wall frames
a A grid for climbing plants can be fixed to the wall with hooks or clamps.
b Anchor battens with wall hooks or eyelets.

should be greater than in a frame intended for plants with tendrils.

Distance from the wall

The climbing support should always be installed at least 5 cm (2 in) from the wall so that the shoots will be able to take enough hold. In addition, air must be able to circulate freely around the plant, to avoid the risk of fungal diseases. Spacers which are easy to install can be obtained in the gardening trade.

What material to use

Structures made of metal are very stable and durable but also rather expensive. They are particularly suited for use as larger, long-term climbing supports. They should be painted, galvanized or plastic-coated to prevent rusting.

Plastic frames are lightweight and durable. The frames should be securely fixed so that they do not get pulled out of shape by the weight of the plant.

Climbing aids made of wood are ideal for many plants. The thickness of the battens should be chosen to cope with the thickness

1 Wire spindles
Plants can be trained into a pyramid shape using this device.

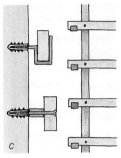

c Insert a grid made of battens into angle irons which have been firmly fixed to the wall with dowels.

and weight of the plant and they should be treated with plant-friendly wood preservative.

An alternative is to paint the entire framework with varnish, making sure to include the parts that will be sunk into the ground.

Climbing aids for containers

● Espalier-like frames made of wire can be obtained in the gardening trade for use with pots and large containers (see illustration 1). Similar frames can be made of bamboo (see illustration 3b). These are simply pushed into the ground.

● Espaliers in various different shapes and sizes are also obtainable for balcony boxes. They can be screwed to the back wall of the box with the help of clamps (see illustration 3a). To prevent the box from tipping over with the weight of the plant, the frame should be attached particularly securely (see p. 18).
● In the case of larger plant containers, a lightweight, mobile espalier can be built quite easily (see illustration 3c). For this you will need bamboo sticks about 2 m (78 in) long and of

two different thicknesses.
Method:
● Using two sticks at a time, cross them at one end and tie them together with strong string. Push the other ends into the corners of the short sides of the plant box (also in the middle of particularly long boxes) using heavy stones to hold them steady.
● Use a thinner bamboo stick to make a cross piece to join the supports at the top.
● Complete the espalier with further, thinner bamboo pieces.

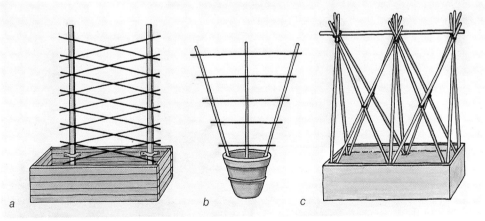

3 Free-standing espaliers for large containers
a A balcony espalier screwed to the back of the wooden box.
b A ready made bamboo espalier for large containers and pots.
c A bamboo frame made of sticks which support each other. Tie them together.

Stylish ideas

Transform your balcony or patio with greenery, allowing your own imagination to inspire you. Whether you decide on an elegant, rustic or Mediterranean style, you will find plenty of ideas here along with breathing examples of plantings in the major popular styles.

Left: *A stair to a patio through wild vine that is beginning to change into its autumn colouring, along with many other hanging and climbing plants in interesting containers.*
Top: *Different containers emphasise the accent of any balcony or patio design.*

Stylish ideas

Traditional designs

By utilizing a few clever tricks you can accomplish quite surprising effects with traditional summer-flowering plants and climbers. These stalwarts of the plant world usually prove completely reliable and will seldom fail to produce healthy foliage and brilliant flowers. The following points should be considered, however, when combining these plants:

● If you want to combine different hanging plants, always check their shape of growth. For example, you can create a splendid effect if you place a plant with a rounded silhouette (like petunias) next to one with long trailing shoots that end in points, like *Plectranthus coleoides* (photo, p. 27).

● Do not combine sparse or slow-growing plants with varieties that grow fast and strong, as the former will end up being smothered by their robust neighbours.

Designing with flowers

The glowing colours and mass of flowers produced by these plants are a great eye-catcher. Usually, the individual flower and its beautiful shape will only really be appreciated when looked at more closely.

These flowers tend to be most effective in a mass as, from a

Plants for particular styles

Permanent plantings
● honeysuckle, ☠
Lonicera henryi
● *Fallopia aubertii*
● wild vine, *Parthenocissus quinquefolia*
● ivy, *Hedera* spp ☠

Rotating plantings
● hanging pelargoniums, *Pelargonium peltatum* hybrids
● hanging fuchsias *Fuchsia* varieties
● hanging begonias, *Begonia* hybrids
● petunias, ☠ *Petunia* hybrids
● busy Lizzies, *Impatiens* hybrids
● *Lobelia erinus*
● black-eyed Susan, *Thunbergia alata*
● *Scaevola saligna*
● alyssum *Lobularia maritima*
● *Sanvitalia procumbens*
● morning glory ☠ *Ipomoea* varieties
● hanging verbenas, *Verbena tenera* hybrids

Container plants
● passion flower, *Passiflora* spp/varieties
● asparagus, *Asparagus densiflorus*

distance, they blend into a single cloud of colour. There are some general rules when using these plants:

● The shades of colour that occur within one species of a plant usually blend together well.

● If you combine two colours, choose more of one than of the other. This will create an interesting balance, more so than if you use equal numbers of plants of each colour.

● The combination of several warm colours, such as yellow, orange and red – or a combination of entirely cool shades, like blue, violet, pink and white, gives a particularly harmonious effect.

● Darker colours emphasize lighter shades.

● A combination of plants in the three primary colours of yellow, red and blue is especially cheerful and bright.

Designing with foliage

Hanging or climbing leafy plants create a pleasant, peaceful effect when grown together with brightly coloured flowers. They will also help to blend colours which normally do not go well together and will help to give structure to a sea of flowers. Ivy (*Hedera* spp) is especially good for this purpose, along with asparagus (*Asparagus* spp) and *Plectranthus* spp or wild vine (*Parthenocissus* spp), *Fallopia aubertii* and honeysuckle

Climbing plants cover the walls of this small patio and create an intimate atmosphere.

(*Lonicera* spp). Even non-flower-ing plants will provide plenty of diversity with their various shades of green, particularly if the autumn colouring of the foliage is interesting.

Containers

Containers made of wood or fired clay are very well suited to traditional planting designs. Plastic containers in neutral, quiet colours or containers made of asbestos-free material are also effective in a rather inconspicu-ous way.

Wild vine in its autumnal colouring.

Stylish ideas

Fuchsias and honeysuckle

This arrangement makes a charming planting. Honeysuckle and mint are able to survive the winter outside, so choose a frost-proof container. The small fuchsia standard should be overwintered indoors. It can be removed from the arrangement and then put back again quite easily the following spring.

Plants for a 60-cm (24 in) diameter container:
2 honeysuckles,
Lonicera x brownii "Fuchsioides",
Lonicera x heckrottii
1 fuchsia standard, *Fuchsia* hybrid
1 hanging spiderwort, *Tradescantia fluminensis*
1 pineapple mint *Mentha suaveolens* "Variegata".
Climbing aid: 3 bamboo sticks (150 cm/60 in long), string or wire. For this planting arrangement, choose a plastic pot with drainage holes, which is large enough to allow the fuchsia standard to fit in loosely.

Position: semi-shade to shady.
Planting and care: Do not plant until after the last frost in the last month of spring, when the choice of fuchsias is greatest. Honeysuckle, mint and *Tradescantia* can be bought at the same time as robust container plants. Fill half of the container with compost and place the two *Lonicera* in the background. In front of them place the empty plastic pot which will later hold the fuchsia standard. Place the *Tradescantia* (renew every year) on the left and the mint on the right so that they hang over the edge of the container. Fill the pot with compost and press it down firmly. Stand the fuchsia in the empty pot and water everything well. Carefully push the three bamboo sticks into the compost between the *Lonicera* plants. The shoots of the honeysuckle should be tied to the sticks every so often during the summer so that the fuchsia does not become smothered.

Fuchsia entwined with other plants and a scented underplanting.

Our tip: Instead of the mint, choose a variegated variety of ivy.

Pelargoniums.

A curtain of pink petunias

The endlessly flowering petunias come in a multitude of different colours. The flowers of the violet "Surfinia" hybrids glow in particularly brilliant shades. They form extremely luxuriant shoots, are weather-hardy and slightly scented.

Plants for a 60-cm (24 in) box:
3 petunias, *Petunia* "Surfinia" hybrids
2 *Plectranthus coleoides*
Position: sunny to semi-shady.
Planting and care: You must use pre-fertilized balcony plant compost. All the plants grow very rapidly and will require a lot of nutrients. The petunias and the *Plectranthus*

Brilliant petunia flowers amid the variegated shoots of Plectranthus coleoides.

should be planted alternately. Stand the box in a very sunny to semi-shady position and water well. Keep evenly moist and fertilize weekly three weeks after planting.

A wire basket.

Clay hanging container.

A half-bowl with a pelargonium
(photo, p. 26 below)

This planting is almost indestructible and will enjoy a very sunny spot that is sheltered from the rain. This arrangement is ideal for decorating the bare walls of a small balcony.

Plants for a half-bowl
30 cm (12 in) in diameter:
1 standard pelargonium, *Pelargonium zonale* hybrid "Bundeskanzler"
1 stonecrop, *Sedum album* "Coral Carpet"

Position: full sunlight.
Planting and care:
Plant the pelargonium at the back and set the *Sedum* at the front, hanging over the edge, then water well.

Stylish ideas

Romantic designs

Here our senses are assailed by colours which glow mysteriously in the dusk and by flowers which release their delicate scent throughout the evening. Climbing and hanging plants can transform a balcony or patio into an enchanted arbour.

Few things can be more relaxing than to sit quietly in the growing dark of evening and enjoy the delightful aroma of flowers and foliage.

Flowers and scents

Before rushing out to buy plants, spend some time studying catalogues or photographs in gardening books. If you wish to create a really "special" effect, you may have to order plants from specialist nurseries.

Colours: Blue is one of the most romantic colours of all. There are many shades to use to create just the right atmosphere. Delicate shades of pink also harmonize extremely well, along with creamy white and palest yellow.
Shapes: It is best to choose delicate flowers, such as bellflower *Campanula poscharskyana* or *Convolvulus sabatius*. Lively, gracious flowers, like those of the sweet pea (*Lathyrus odoratus*), also suit this arrangement very well.

Suitable plants

You must remember to give thought to colours of flowers and foliage as well as shapes and scent. You must also take into consideration the colours and shapes of your balcony or patio furniture.

Permanent plantings
● *Clematis* hybrids
● climbing roses, *Rosa* varieties

Alternating plantings
Erigeron karvinskianus
Convolvulus sabatius
Saevola saligna
Brachycome iberidifolia
● sweet pea, ☠
Lathyrus odoratus
Campanula poscharskyana
Plectranthus coleoides
Eccremocarpus scaber
Tropaeolum peregrinum
Asarina barclaiana
● morning glory, ☠
Ipomoea tricolor
Lobelia erinus

Container plants
Plumbago auriculata
Trachelospermum jasminoides
Centradenia "Cascade"

Scent: A corner to sit out in is best enjoyed at dusk. Delicate scents serve only to enhance the romantic effect. The following plants have light, pleasant scents:
● *Brachycome iberidifolia*
● heliotrope, cherry pie *Heliotropium arborescens*
● sweet pea *Lathyrus odoratus*
● *Lobularia maritima*
● scented pelargoniums, which are also well suited to hanging baskets: *Pelargonium x fragrans* (scent of pine), *Pelargonium x fragrans* "Lilian Pottinger" (scent of pineapple), *Pelargonium odoratissimum* (lemon-apple scent), *Pelargonium crispum* "Minor" (lemon scent)
● *Trachelospermum jasminoides*

Decorative foliage

Colours: Creamy shades of green are especially suitable - bright green would destroy the subtle, delicate effect. Foliage in shades of blue green or smoky grey will enhance the atmosphere and the same goes for the dainty, greenish-white leaves of *Plectranthus coleoides*.
Shapes: Choose small, delicate, ornamental-leaved species and varieties. Very large leaves do not create a romantic image.

Flowers in delicate shades of blue have transformed this patio.

Containers and climbing aids

Glazed or unglazed clay pots with dainty ornamentation are well suited to the romantic style. Blue or cream coloured tubs also harmonize well. Climbing supports made of wood are suitable, as are various other materials. The wood can be painted in suitable colours. Even simple sticks or branches can be employed. Before planting, draw a plan of your arrangement on paper and shade in the colours you are aiming for in crayon. Be critical. Is the result too bland, too one-sided? Move the arrangement about on paper until you are pleased with it.

Clematis "Durandii".

Stylish ideas

Decorative screens

Annuals with tendrils are busy climbers. During their short vege-tation period – from the last month of spring to the first frosts in the second month of autumn, they manage to produce a consider-able amount of foliage. Their delicate shoots and tendrils climb to dizzying heights and may be covered in colourful flowers all summer long. In the shortest possible time these charming plants will ensure complete privacy and seclusion.

A charming composition in which annual plants entwine.

Plants for 60-cm (24 in) diamter boxes:
3 canary creepers
Tropaeolum peregrinum
1 nasturtium,
Tropaeolum majus

1 *Eccremocarpus scaber*
1 *Asarina barclaiana*
Climbing aids: 10 thin bamboo sticks (70 cm/28 in long), string or wire.

Planting and care: You can buy all of these plants during the last month of spring or grow them from seed from the middle of the sec-ond month of spring (see propagation, p. 52). Space out the plants alternately in the box, press the compost down and water. Push the sticks into the box side by side so that every two cross in the middle, then tie them. To begin with, train the tendrils in the desired direction of growth and carefully fasten them

with twine or string. Tendrils which tend to spread out a great deal should be bent back towards the support and tied up so that they form a dense screen. Fertilize weekly.
Position: sunny to semi-shady.
Alternative: If you use old, dead branches without leaves instead of the bamboo sticks, the effect created will be like an enchanted hedgerow. Set the branches close together in the soil or compost in the box.

Eccremocarpus scaber.

Tropaeolum peregrinum.

My tip: Plastic support sticks or asbestos-free boxes can be varnished in any colour. Shades of blue make a particularly attractive contrast to the colours of the flowers of annual climbing plants.

An espalier plant grouping

This is a romantic arrangement which comes into its own during the hours of dusk. The colours of the flowers seem to glow in the half-light of evening.

Container plants
You will need a container 60 cm (24 in) long, 40 cm (16 in) wide, 25 cm (10 in) tall:
1 *Clematis* hybrid
1 *Pharbitis purpurea*
1 heliotrope, *Heliotropium arborescens*
2 petunias, *Petunia* hybrids
2 *Erigeron karvinskianus*.
Climbing aids: 1 wooden espalier (at least 100 cm/40 in tall), varnished green.
Position: sunny to semi-shady.
Planting and care: Use

A decorative screen.

a frost-proof container, as the *Clematis* will be able to survive the winter outside in a sheltered position. All the other plants are annuals and have to be renewed every year.
Buy the plants in the last month of spring. The espalier should be placed inside the box

A terracotta container.

against the back wall (it can be fixed with screws in a wooden box, see illustration, p. 21). Fill a third of the container with compost. Place the *Clematis* close to the espalier in the background to the left, then add the *Pharbitis* to the right with some space between. Plant the *Erigeron* and the petunias at the front so that they hang over the edge, and place the *Heliotropium* immediately behind them. Add more compost between the plants and water well.

Our tip: Prevent the espalier wood from rotting after one year by painting it thoroughly with wood preservative beforehand, especially the parts that will end up underground.

Stylish ideas

A classical design

Handsome flowers, delicate colours, graceful tendrils and striking leaves will add a touch of classical elegance to any balcony or patio. The impressive over-hanging leaves of *Chlorophytum comosum* or the bizarre-shaped, branching, climbing shoots of many ivy species (*Hedera*) char-acterize this style.

The most suitable plants are those which openly display every single shoot and leaf and do not hide them in a restless welter of flowers and leaves.

A harmonious flower display

Colours: The colour of a flower can create a warm effect or look cold. All cool shades go well with the classical style and these include the entire palette of colours from blue to violet to bluish-red. White or dark, almost blackish, flowers also belong in this category, not to forget the enchanting shades of pastel colours, e.g. light blue, lilac, pink or apricot.

Shapes: Use plants with large, broad flower shapes, like the climbing rose (*Rosa* spp) or *Clematis* hybrids. Small, delicate-looking flowers, like those of the fuchsia (*Fuchsia* hybrids) or *Rhodochiton atrosanguineus*, also go well with the classical style.

Suitable plants for a classical planting design

Permanent planting
● climbing roses,
Rosa spp/varieties
● *Clematis* hybrids ☠
● ivy, *Hedera* spp ☠
● wisteria, ☠
Wisteria sinensis
● *Aristolochia macrophylla*
● *Santolina chamaecyparis-sus*

Alternating planting
● hanging pelargoniums,
Pelargonium peltatum hybrids
● hanging fuchsias
Fuchsia hybrids
● *Cobaea scandens*
● morning glory, ☠
Ipomoea tricolor
● *Rhodochiton atrosan-guineus*
● *Scaevola saligna*
● *Lotus berthelottii,*
Lotus maculatus "Golden Flash"

Container plants
● *Pandorea jasminoides*
● *Mandevilla laxa*
● passion flower
Passiflora spp/varieties

Interesting leaves

Colours: Foliage in shades of blue green suit the classical theme best; yellow green should be avoided. Grey foliage, like that of lavender (*Lavandula angustifo-lia*) or *Calocephalus brownii*, emphasizes the mood of this style, as do the dark, brownish-red leaves of *Heuchera san-guinea*. An arresting note is pro-vided by plants with interesting leaf markings. Ivy varieties (*Hedera* spp) with white-edged leaves are just one example.
Shapes: Choose plants with large leaves or leaves with sim-ple, geometric shapes.

The final effect

Obviously, there is no point in creating a classical design through the use of atmospheric foliage if the subtle effect you have so painstakingly created will be ruined by brightly coloured patio or balcony furniture or a background wall painted in a bright summer colour. Before planting, do try to stand back and imagine the final result from a distance. This could save a lot of hard work and disappoint-ment.

Wrought-iron furniture and clearly defined leaf shapes create an elegant classical style.

Containers and climbing aids

The material out of which the containers are made is not quite so important for the classical style. It is their colours, surface structure and shape that are far more important. Shiny containers in shades of white, grey or black, in classical, geometric shapes are particularly suitable.

Containers made of clay or wood with a slightly whitish glaze appear restrained. Annual, rapidly growing climbing plants will quickly obscure any climbing frame or structure and render it "invisible". In the case of perennials or slow-growing plants, white or dark green painted espaliers made of wood or metal look very elegant.

A garden seat entwined with ivy.

Stylish ideas

Scented roses and golden green ivy

Hardy climbers combined with pendulous summer flowers.

Plants for large containers with a diameter of 60 cm (24 in):
1 continuously flowering climbing rose, variety "Ramira"
1 ivy, *Hedera helix* "Goldheart"
1 coral flower, *Heuchera* hybrid "Palace Purple"
1 *Scaevola saligna*
1 *Brachycome iberidifolia*
1 *Calocephalus brownii*
1 *Santolina chamaecyparissus*
Climbing aid: 1 wire mesh painted white, 60 cm (24 in) wide, 100 cm (40 in) long; 2 bamboo sticks, 100 cm (40 in) long; wire for tying.
Position: sunny to semi-shady.
Planting and care: This planting arrangement will look decorative even during the winter, so choose a frost-proof container.
Fill the container half-full of compost. Plant the ivy 15 cm (6 in) from the back edge and to the

Attractively marked ivy leaves and roses combine in handsome elegance.

34

left and place the rose to the right. In front, plant the *Heuchera* and the *Santolina*. Then add the underplanting of *Scaevola, Brachycome* and *Calocephalus* towards the front so that they hang over the edges. Drive in a bamboo stick behind the ivy and the rose, close to the edge of the container. Tie the wire mesh tightly to the sticks with wire. Water well and keep evenly moist. Keep tying the ivy to the wire mesh.

Overwintering tip: The rose, ivy, *Heuchera* and *Santolina* are hardy. Protect these plants with dry bracken or brushwood and water them in winter during frost-free days. The other plants, *Scaevola, Brachycome* and *Calocephalus*, are annuals and will have to be replaced every year, either with the same or other plants.

A flowering fountain in delicate pastel shades

This creates an overflowing mass of flowers and foliage all summer

A flowering waterfall for a semi-shady corner.

long, even in shadier positions.

Plants for a bowl with a diameter of 30 cm (12 in):
1 *Rhodochiton atrosanguineus*
1 ivy with white-green leaves, *Hedera* variety
1 *Chlorophytum comosum*

1 hanging begonia, *Begonia* – tuber begonia hybrid, *Flore pleno pendula* hybrid

Position: semi-shade to shade.

Planting and care: Buy the plants in the last month of spring. Place the *Chlorophytum* in the background, with the other plants in front. Make sure that the plants do not become waterlogged after watering, as both the *Chlorophytum* and the *Begonia* are particularly sensitive to wetness.

Designer tip: Plants with long shoots and tendrils look particularly elegant on a decorative pedestal. Their beautiful hanging foliage will be set off really well in such an arrangement.

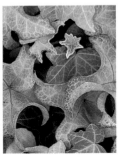

The elegance of ivy.

Stylish ideas

Rustic designs

A balcony or patio can be transformed into a rustic paradise if you use the appropriate flowers and foliage. Everything can be allowed to mix together in a colourful mass. Another pleasing feature of a rustic garden is growing soft fruit, vegetables and herbs among the flowering plants. Allow your imagination to take over. Two typical representatives of a rustic garden, sunflowers (*Helianthus annuus*) and hollyhocks (*Alcea rosea*), will attain heights of up to 2 m (80 in) in a large container. So, how about planting sunflowers, for example, with red-flowering runner beans climbing up them? This will involve growing the sunflowers earlier, as they will need a good start to prevent the fast-growing beans from catching up and overtaking them! As with all planting experiments, the plants should always blend together from the point of view of colour, shape and effect.

Rustic flowers

Colours: Whether you prefer a mass of different colours or wish to create a particular colour scheme, you can simply follow your own taste with this style. In most cottage gardens, flowers are allowed to mix happily together, although you will find that some colours tend to pre-

Suitable plants

Permanent planting
- box, ☠
  Buxus sempervirens
- *Campanula poscharskyana*
- Russian vine,
  Fallopia aubertii
- honeysuckle, ☠
  Lonicera caprifolium
- climbing roses,
  Rosa varieties

Alternate planting
- slipper flower,
  Calceolaria integrifolia
- petunias, ☠
  Petunia hybrids
- hanging pelargoniums,
  Pelargonium peltatum hybrids
- nasturtiums,
  Tropaeolum majus
- runner bean,
  Phaseolus coccineus
- *Begonia limmingheana*
- black-eyed Susan,
  Thunbergia alata
- sweet pea, ☠
  Lathyrus odoratus
- hanging fuchsia,
  Fuchsia varieties
- *Erigeron karvinskianus*
- *Sanvitalia procumbens*

Container plants
- asparagus
  Asparagus densiflorus

dominate. Certain features should be taken into consideration when combining colours: bluish-red will clash with yellow or orange but white will go with anything and tends to have a neutralizing effect.

Shapes: Plants with single, simple flowers, like *Erigeron karvinskianus*, the small-flowered *Campanula poscharskyana* and *Centradenia* "Cascade", which only really show their total charm when massed together, are all suitable for this style.

Alternatively, you may wish to choose lively, broad, round flowers like petunias, begonias or roses. They can be placed together with more complicated flower structures, e.g. sweet peas (*Lathyrus odoratus*) and still look splendid.

A variety of leaves

Colours: Anything you fancy is allowed. Experiment with the most varied colours of leaves! Try creating beautiful contrasts by combining grey leaves, for example, with those of *Lotus berthelottii* or *Lotus maculatus*, or with *Senecio* which neither rambles nor climbs but is popularly used in rustic gardens in various combinations.

Forms of leaves: Again, you can experiment and combine entirely according to your own taste. Interesting effects can be obtained by placing plants with

With its lavender blue, star-shaped flowers, bellflower (Campanula poscharskyana) is ideal for a patio with a retaining wall.

large leaves next to more delicately formed ones.

Containers and climbing aids

Smooth, simple clay pots will suit a rustic arrangement just as well as boxes made of wood. Baskets give a very rustic effect, although they should be propped up on two small wooden battens, otherwise there is a tendency for the basket to decay rather quickly. Climbing aids made of wood and wire mesh look good with the rustic style. Pots and tubs that will take on a "weathered" look are very suitable.

A climbing aid made of wood.

Stylish ideas

Pretty little flower faces will liven up the winter green of box throughout the entire summer (photo, right).

Plants for a bowl with a diameter of 60 cm (24 in) and at least 20 cm (8 in) tall:
1 spherical box shrub (diameter of the globe 35 cm or 14 in), *Buxus sempervirens*
2 black-eyed Susan, *Thunbergia alata*
3 hanging *Campanula poscharskyana*
Position: sunny to semi-shady.
Planting and care: Use a frost-proof container. Place the box shrub in the background and the two *Thunbergia* to the right in front.
In the foreground, plant the *Campanula*, allowing them to hang over the edge of the container. Water well and keep the bowl evenly moist. During the winter, place the bowl in a sheltered position and water it on frost-free days. The black-eyed Susan will have to be replaced every year.

Hanging baskets have a long tradition in Britain (photo, p. 39 right).

Plants for a wire basket with a diameter of 40 cm (16 in):
2 *Petunia* hybrids
2 hanging pelargoniums, *Pelargonium peltatum* hybrids
3 *Bidens ferulifolia*
3 nasturtiums, *Tropaeolum majus*
2 *Lobelia erinus*
2 *Lotus maculatus*
Accessories: 1 thick wad of moss (this can sometimes be found in the lawn) or substitute coconut fibre (from a garden centre), or wood shavings.
Position: sunny to semi-shady.
Planting and care: Hang the basket at chest height, line the

A cahrming display of flowers and box.

A willow basket.

An oak wood container.

inside with moss, then place polythene sheeting over this.
Plant from the bottom upwards. Cut openings in the moss and sheeting. From the outside, carefully push the plant rootstocks through the wire mesh, moss and polythene to the beginning of the stalks, then

close the hole with more moss. Disperse half of the plants in the lower part of the basket. Then fill the basket with compost so that all the rootstocks are covered, and press down. The upper half of the basket should be planted in the same way.

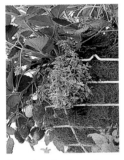

Strawberries in a wire basket. This arrangement not only looks pretty – you can also eat the results!

Water the basket thoroughly, then water daily (twice on hot days) and fertilize weekly.

My tip: Stand a basin or bowl underneath to catch the water that runs out!

A hanging basket with cheerful flowers.

Stylish ideas

Mediterranean arrangements

Growing flowers in large containers is very popular in Mediterranean and subtropical regions. Even in Europe, however, balconies and patios can be transformed into a holiday paradise quite simply. Breathtakingly beautiful flowers, glorious colours and intoxicating scents are the characteristics of Mediterranean plants. All of them require a great deal of sunlight and plenty of warmth. Sunshine really brings out their brilliant colours and makes them glow. Remember that you do not have to remain rigidly purist about these matters! Just go ahead and choose tropical plants that you like for your sunlit balcony.

Colour and scent

Brilliant, pure colours, like blue, red, yellow and orange, are the characteristic colours of the Mediterranean. Delicate shades are not right for this style, as they lose much of their effect in strong sunlight. Many scents are inextricably bound up with memories of holidays in the south, like the scent of lemons (*Citrus limon*) and Seville orange (*Citrus aurantium*), which can be grown in large containers.
The aromatic scent of thyme (*Thymus* spp) alone can conjure up a holiday atmosphere.

Suitable plants for a Mediterranean arrangement

Permanent plantings
● grapevine, *Vitis vinifera*
● *Santolina chamaecyoparissus*
● *Campsis x tagliabuana*

Alternate plantings
● jasmine,
Jasminum officinale
● *Echevaria carnicolor*
● *Sedum morganianum*
● *Portulaca grandiflora*
● hanging pelargonium,
Pelargonium peltatum hybrid
● hanging fuchsia,
Fuchsia varieties
● *Scaevola saligna*
● hanging verbena,
Verbena tenera hybrids
● *Brachycome iberidifolia*
● *Quamoclit lobata* ☠

Container plants
● passion flower,
Passiflora caerulea
● *Bougainvillea* species
● *Plumbago auriculata*
● *Podranea ricasoliana*
● white nightshade, ☠
Solanum jasminoides

Flowers and leaves

Shapes of flowers: Plants with exotic flower shapes are right for this style. They may be large flowers, like those of *Bougainvillea* species and passion flower (*Passiflora caerulea*), or even small ones, like those of jasmine (*Jasminum officinale*) and *Trachelspermum jasminoides*.
Colours of leaves: Many typical Mediterranean plants produce juicy green leaves. However, there are also grey green shades, like the foliage of *Santolina chamaecyparissus*, which provide attractive contrasts.
Shapes of leaves:
Mediterranean plants protect themselves against water loss through evaporation from their leaves with various "tricks". Strong, small leaves which are covered in a shiny layer of wax will lose less water (*Citrus* spp). Small, fleshy, thick leaves, like those of *Sedum* species are even able to store water.

Our tip: Plants in large containers can attain a considerable height, just think of the olive tree (*Olea europea*), oleander (*Nerium oleander*), hibiscus (*Hibiscus rosa-sinensis*) or the various *Citrus* species. Hanging plants are an ideal underplanting as they provide shade for the root area of a plant in a large container (photo above).

Hanging plants with citrus trees. Here, Lotus maculatus and Bougainvillea form enchanting underplantings.

Containers and climbing aids

Containers made of reddish terracotta are typical of Mediterranean gardens, and they should, if possible, be decorated with ornamentation. However, even plant containers made of stone can give a balcony or patio that certain southern flair. Climbing supports made of bamboo or wood are particularly suitable. Make sure that any furniture or accessories on your patio or balcony will complement the atmosphere you intend to create.

Bougainvillea.

A hint of the south

To create a holiday mood on your balcony or patio, combine the shimmering sea green of juniper, a firework display of red *Campsis* and the light-coloured flowering stars of passion flower (*Passiflora caerulea*). All of these southern beauties are easy to care for and, with the exception of passion flower, all are hardy.

Plants for a container with a diameter of 70 cm (28 cm):
1 *Campsis x tagliabuana*,
1 juniper,
Juniperus squamata
1 passion flower,
Passiflora caerulea
1 *Sedum floriferum*
1 *Santolina chamaecyparissus*
Climbing aids: 2 thick bamboo sticks, 200 cm (80 in) long; 3 bamboo sticks, 100 cm (40 in) long; string for tying.
Accessories: 1 plastic pot with drainage holes (the pot of *Passiflora* should fit loosely into it).
Position: sunny to semi-shady.
Planting and care:
You will need to choose

The profusely flowering Campsis grows tall.

Campsis x tagliabuana.

a frost-proof container. The best planting time is during the second month of spring. Fill the container half-full of potting compost. The climbing aid should be shaped like a ladder. Drive two 200 cm (80 in) long bamboo sticks into the compost in the back third of the pot,

each set close to the left and right of the pot wall. Use the three short bamboo sticks as cross bars, spacing them well apart and tying them tightly with wire to the longer sticks. Place the *Campsis* in front of the sticks and tie the shoots to them. Plant the juniper at the front, slanting forward over the edge of the pot. Place the larger, empty plastic pot behind the juniper (this is reserved for the passion flower), then place the remaining plants in the spaces between. Fill the remainder of the pot with compost and press down. Water well. In the last month of spring, place the passion flower (in its pot) in the built-in plastic pot.

Overwintering tips:
The passion flower is not hardy and should, therefore, be cut back before the first frost, taken out and overwintered indoors in a bright position at about 10°C (50°F). All other plants can overwinter outside in a sheltered position and covered with brushwood.
They should be watered on frost-free days.

During the last month of winter, cut off all the deadheads of the *Campsis* and remove any dead wood. The plant will produce new flowers on the newly forming shoots.

Your own grape harvest

There is no need to travel to warmer climes for the autumnal grape harvest. If you plant a grapevine in a container on your balcony, you may be able to harvest bunches of luscious fruit right there on your own doorstep. This vine is fairly undemanding and can be kept for years in a position well sheltered from the wind.

Plants for a container with a diameter of 50 cm (20 in), 50 cm (20 in) wide and 40 cm (16 in) high:

1 grapevine, *Vitis vinifera*
4 thyme plants, *Thymus doerfleri* "Bressingham Seedling"
Climbing aids:
1 wooden stake; string for tying.
Position: sunny.
Planting and care: The

This grapevine requires plenty of sunlight.

best time to plant is in spring. Make sure you choose strong healthy plants when purchasing. Choose a frost-proof container and use nutrient-rich, sandy-loamy soil. Fill the container half-full of soil and plant the grapevine in it. Fill the container with more soil and care-

fully insert the wooden stake between the root-stock and the back wall of the container. Tie the vine to it. Plant the thyme plants all round the vine. They will develop into a dense cushion with a delicate, aromatic scent. Water well and keep the soil evenly moist. During the summer, fertilize once a month with mineral fertilizer. Cut back the vine to a few shoots in the first month of winter and provide some form of winter protection.

Our tip: The following types of vines are suitable for cooler positions:
● "Weisser Gutedel"
● "Roter Gutedel"
● "Früher Malinger"
● "Früher Blauer Burgunder"

Harvest time.

Successful plant care

All plants will require the right sort of care
if you wish your balcony or patio to
become a successful "garden". The following pages will tell you what you need
to know to look after them.

Left: *Enchanting wisteria. If you wish to grow this
abundantly flowering plant all over a pergola, plant
it in the garden soil, not in a large container.*
Above: *The continual-flowering climbing rose
"Ramira".*

Successful plant care

Choice and planting

Your chances of success will be much improved if you choose the right plants and learn how to plant them in groups.
● Only choose plants that will suit the position of your balcony or patio and its lighting conditions (sun, semi-shade, shade).
● If you have a small balcony, do not choose plants which grow fast and abundantly as it will be difficult to keep them in check.
● Only choose plants which correspond to the colour and style of your design scheme.

Care of containers

It is not only your plants that will need care and attention, pots, boxes and hanging containers also need regular care.
● Before planting, clean the containers thoroughly and brush them off. Also soak clay containers well.
● Any lime residue can be removed with a vinegar and water solution.
● If the previous plant was diseased, the container should also be cleaned with a disinfectant.
● Glazed and painted containers should be checked for cracks and splits and, if necessary, receive a new coat of paint.

Watering

Plants need water to live just as much as humans and animals. With the help of water, the roots absorb nutrients and transport them to the vascular tissue and then on to the furthest shoot tips and leaves. Climbing plants in particular often have extremely long shoots so that the distances from roots to shoot tips are quite considerable. Regular watering is therefore extremely important in dry summers.
● Do not water too often, but always do so very thoroughly.
● Freshly planted plants will require more frequent watering.
● Never water during the daytime while the sun is shining.
● Water evergreen plants thoroughly in the autumn and on frost-free days during the winter. They will lose water through evaporation, which they cannot replenish from the soil.
● Plants in boxes, pots or containers should not be watered to death. Here, too, water less frequently but thoroughly if the soil is still dry a few centimetres below the surface.

Our tip: Remember that climbing plants along house walls or in hanging baskets under balconies and rooftops usually do not receive any rainwater.

Fertilizing

In addition to water, nutrients also play an important role in the well-being of plants. The plants can only develop properly if all the nutrients they need for growing are available in the soil. A distinction is made between macronutrients which plants require in large quantities (nitrogen, phosphorous, potassium, calcium, sulphur and magnesium) and trace elements which are effective in very small doses (like iron, zinc, copper, manganese and others). Fertilize plants in containers with compound fertilizer. This contains the main nutrients and trace elements in balanced, plant-friendly ratios.

The most important points when fertilizing

● From the last month of spring to the first month of autumn, annual hanging and climbing plants should be provided with a weekly dose of liquid fertilizer mixed in with their water. (Special tips on fertilizing, see p. 11.)
● Perennial hanging and climbing plants in containers should be lightly fertilized at fortnightly intervals from the last month of spring until the last month of summer.
Cease fertilizing at the end of the last month of summer so that the shoots will be able to mature

Like a brocade carpet - wild vine and flowering ivy (Hedera helix "Arborescens").

before you take the plants inside during the autumn.

Organic or mineral fertilizer?

Organic fertilizers, like ripe compost or well-rotted manure, are especially recommended for perennial plants planted outside. During the autumn, the soil around the plants can be covered with a layer of this type of fertilizer. Occasionally, horn chips and bone meal should also be worked into the soil. These are good for a regular supply of trace elements. Further fertilization is not generally necessary for perennial species that are planted outside.

Mineral fertilizers are rapidly absorbed by plants and quickly become effective. They are recommended for annual plants grown in containers during their flowering period or whenever they are seen to be suffering from an acute lack of nutrients. Always follow the instructions meticulously. Use mineral fertilizer very sparingly for climbing plants planted outside.

General care

Rules for pruning woody plants

Some perennial climbing plants are cut back to check excessive growth, to encourage the growth of shoots and the formation of flowers or to rejuvenate them (see table, p. 50). In principle, the same rules apply to them all:
● First, remove all old and dead branches.
● Cut out branches growing across each other.
● The edge of the cut should always be slightly slanted, to prevent rainwater from collecting on the cut and increasing the risk of infection.
● Wounds which are wider than a thumbnail should always be treated with a wound-sealing agent.
● Keep your cutting tools well sharpened so that the cuts are clean.
● Make sure your tools are clean. Always disinfect the tools after cutting diseased plants.

Our tip: Never dispose of the cut-off parts of diseased plants on your compost heap! Burn them or put them in your household refuse.

The right way to prune
(see illustration 1)

The cut should be made about 5 mm above the bud, often called the "eye" by gardeners. Make sure that you never cut towards the bud (see illustration 1c) but always sloping away from the it (see illustration 1d). If the cut is too low (see illustration 1b), the bud will wither and not produce a shoot. If it is too high (see illustration 1a) the bud will not shoot.

Tying up shoots
(see illustration 2)

Most climbing plants should be trained on a support and tied up. A few self-climbers, like ivy (*Hedera* spp) or wild vine (*Parthenocissus*), and plants with tendrils, which support themselves, will not require tying. The most impor-

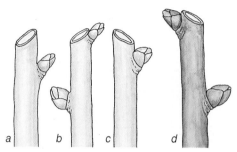

1 The right and wrong ways to prune
Wrong: a The space above the bud is too great; b Too small; c The cut is made towards the bud. **Correct:** *d Cut 5 mm above the bud and downwards and away from it.*

tant thing is to make sure that the shoots of young plants in particular and species which do not become woody are not tied up too tightly and thus become constricted.
The best thing to do is to tie the plant loosely to the climbing aid with garden raffia or hemp rope, forming a figure-of-eight loop (see illustration 2a). Plastic-coated wire is also suitable. It should be wound loosely around the

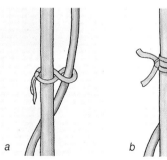

2 Tying plants to a support stick
a A figure-of-eight loop made of raffia or hemp rope.
b A loose tie of plastic-coated wire.

shoot and knotted behind the climbing aid (see illustration 2b).

Tidying the plant

Deadheads and dead leaves should be regularly cut off and cleared away, particularly with annual flowering plants. This will prevent the formation of seeds which represents a great loss of energy for the plant and is generally detrimental to the formation of further flowers. However, the faded flowers of species which are planted for their fruits as well as their flowers, like runner beans (*Phaseolus coccineus*), kiwi fruit (*Actinidia chinensis*) or

4 Immersing a hanging container
Immerse the rootstock and container in water.

Pyracantha species, should be left untouched.

Watering hanging containers

(see illustrations 3 and 4)

Shower accessory: Providing plants in hanging containers with water is a little more difficult than with plants in boxes and large containers. If the hanging container is so heavy that you cannot take it down every time you want to water it, a shower attachment is a good idea (see illustration 3). This shower head attachment on the end of a piece of plastic tube is simply fixed to an ordinary garden hose.

Pumping can: Special watering cans with a pump action for watering hanging containers are obtainable in the gardening trade. These cans allow the water to be pumped up into the hanging container by means of a pipe.

Immersing: A further possibility for watering hanging containers is immersing them (see

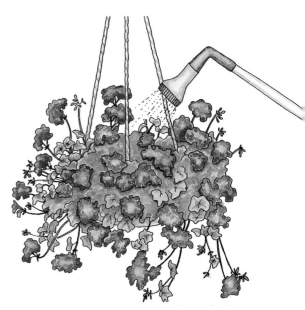

3 Watering a hanging container with a shower attachment
These special attachments for garden hoses are available in the gardening trade.

illustration 4, left). For this purpose, remove the hanging container and immerse the rootstock in a bucket or bath filled with tepid water until no more tiny bubbles are seen rising to the surface of the water.

Pulley: In the case of very heavy hanging containers, you may wish to set up a rope and pulley which will facilitate taking down

the container for watering purposes.

This also makes deadheading and other plant care easier as you do not have to stretch up or stand on a ladder and you can see exactly what you are doing all round the container, not just at the front.

Successful plant care

Cutting back perennial climbing plants

Plant	Tips on pruning
Campsis spp	Shoots from the previous year are cut back.
Clematis hybrids early flowering	Regular cutting back. Not at all, or cut back after the main flowering period.
late flowering	Prune in early spring.
Clematis, wild spp	Not at all, or only a little.
Fallopia spp	An annual pruning in early spring will prevent the tendency to produce bare branches.
Humulus lupulus hops	In late autumn or early spring cut off just above the surface of the ground.
Jasminum nudiflorum winter jasmine	Occasionally cut back after flowering.
Lonicera spp honeysuckle	Occasionally cutting back after flowering will prevent bareness.
Parthenocissus spp wild vine	It is possible to cut back to check excessive growth.
Rosa spp climbing roses: once-flowering continuous-flowering	Annual pruning; cut off deadheads with two leaves. Prune after flowering. Prune during the second month of spring.
Vitis vinifera grape vine	An annual pruning in early spring.
Wisteria spp wisteria	Cut back, to check growth and encourage flower formation, in early spring and summer.

Evergreen climbing plants

Even in winter, by using evergreen plants it is possible to create pleasing splashes of colour on a wall or in containers. Suitable species include:

● Spindleberry (*Euonymus fortunei*). Several species of this plant, which has rooting suckers and very attractively coloured leaves, can be obtained, such as "Vegetus", "Coloratus" or "Gracilis". Some of them will require help in climbing.

● Ivy (*Hedera* spp and varieties). The best known is *Hedera helix*. You can also obtain *Hedera hibernica* (not quite so hardy) and *Hedera colchica*. *Hedera helix* "Baltica" and "Helvetica" are particularly hardy. Some varieties have white or variegated foliage.

● Climbing blackberry (*Rubus henryi*). This evergreen rambler is only hardy in regions with a mild climate and in sheltered positions. It is best to give it some form of winter protection. The plant can be cut back without problems after damage by frost.

Winter protection for climbing and hanging plants

Most perennial climbing plants are sufficiently hardy and will not require any special winter protection. Some very sensitive species will, however, only survive without protection in mild regions. In harsher climates they will need protection (see illustration, right).

Boxes and large containers which will remain outside with the plants in them should be covered with brushwood. In particularly draughty positions, the containers can also be wrapped in polystyrene, bubble pack, sacking or newspaper.

Hanging containers are best removed and overwintered indoors, in a warm or cool place, depending on their species (see table, pp. 10-11). Containers which are emptied for the duration of the winter should be thoroughly cleaned out.

Our tip: Remember that large containers or boxes including plants and climbing structures are very heavy and can be difficult to move about. A trolley of some kind, with rollers, is very useful. If the container is made of wood, you can screw rollers straight on to it.

Overwintering plants outside

Plants on a supporting structure

Plants which are sensitive to frost, like some of the climbing roses (*Rosa* varieties), *Campsis* species or kiwi fruit (*Actinidia chinensis*), will require winter protection, particularly in regions with a less mild climate. If they are planted in boxes, these should be packed in polystyrene sheets and set on two pieces of wood. The plants themselves can be protected with reed mats.

Covering a box

If the plants in containers are hardy, they can remain on the balcony or patio and simply be protected with a covering of brushwood.

Protection for species and varieties planted outside

In the case of frost-sensitive plants that are planted in beds outside, scatter mature compost, bark mulch or dead leaves around the roots. This will improve the soil and protect the plants from frost. Wrap reed or straw mats around the plant. They will shield it from frost and the drying effects of sunshine. The mats can be removed on frost-free days. Remember to remove the winter protection in good time when the weather gets warmer, otherwise the plants will start shooting under the protective covering and the shoots will turn yellow because they receive no sunlight.

Propagating

Seed
(see illustration 1)

Many annual climbing and hanging plants are easily grown from seed. Seed for most annuals can be obtained in the gardening trade. In the case of annuals, start sowing as early as the last month of winter, so that your plants will flower as early as possible. For this purpose, you will require transparent covering or a small propagator, as well as seeding compost. This compost is not pre-fertilized and is particularly loose and free of weed seeds. You can also mix it yourself out of peat and sand in a ratio of 1:1.

NB: Only fresh seeds will germinate reliably!

Method
● Fill the seed tray with seeding compost.
● Scatter the seeds evenly and not too close together. Large seeds should be inserted into the compost individually.
● Water with a fine spray.
● Cover the tray well. Stand on a bright, warm window ledge.
● Check occasionally to see if the compost has dried out. Moisten, if necessary.
● As soon as the first leaves show, open up the cover a little, to prevent the formation of fungi.

Pricking out seedlings
(illustration 2)

The fast-growing young plants need enough room to develop. Any weak seedlings should be removed, or else plant the larger seedlings in new containers. This should not be done too late, otherwise disentangling the roots will become difficult. Prick out when the seedlings possess two pairs of leaves or look too close together.

Method
● Loosen the soil around the little plants. Carefully lift out the seedlings by their leaves and replant them in small pots or seed trays. Use lightly fertilized pricking-out compost or flower compost mixed with additional sand.
● The pricked-out plants should be placed in a bright position and will no longer require a cover.
● The young plants can be planted outside after the last frosts, about the middle of the third month of spring.

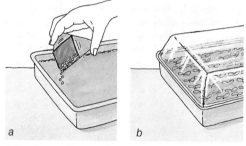

1 Sowing a *Scatter the seeds evenly.*
b *Keep the tray humid and warm with a cover.*

2 Pricking out *Carefully lift the seedlings out of the compost and replant them.*

Propagating from cuttings

(see illustration 3)

Cuttings can be taken from many perennial hanging and climbing plants. They should root well and grow into new plants. Cuttings are especially suitable if you wish to propagate particular varieties that do not always come true with seeds. They can be taken during the entire growth period, from spring to autumn. Use the tips of shoots

that have not yet turned woody, as they form roots more readily.

Method
● Cut off the shoots with a sharp knife just beneath a leaf.
● Remove the lower leaves so that they will not decay.
● Plant the shoot in a pot of compost at a depth of 2-3 cm (1 in). Flower compost mixed with sand is a suitable medium.
● After watering, cover the pot with a transparent plastic hood pulled over a wire loop. This will create high humidity and the plant will require less water.

Our tip: The pot should be placed in a warm position to encourage the growth of roots (about 20°C/68°F).

● Remove the hood if new leaves appear or the shoot begins to grow.

3 Cuttings from shoot tips
a Cut off the shoot at a slant directly under a leaf.
b Remove the lower leaves, plant the shoot and water.
c Bend the wire into a loop. Pull a plastic bag over it. Tie the bag tight.

Pinching out shoot tips

(see illustration 4)

Most climbing plants first form long shoots with few leaves, in order to reach the light as quickly as possible. Then these begin to branch out at the ends and start to flower. You should, however, encourage your plants to produce branches on the lower parts of the shoots if you want to obtain dense foliage

and abundant flowers. To obtain this result, you will have to keep on pinching out the shoot tips of the young plants with your fingers. This encourages the formation of many lateral shoots.

4 Pinching out
Pinch out the shoot tips.

Successful plant care

An elegant combination of decorative foliage and pastel-coloured flowers.

Prevention of damage to plants

Most plants will prove robust and resistant to disease if they are provided with the best possible living conditions. Few species make enough demands to be considered "difficult". Damage can be caused through mistakes made in caring for plants, such as not recognizing the requirements of an individual species when watering or fertilizing or repotting the plant too late. Pests will appear if the plants are grown in unsuitable compost or if their position is not favourable (see p. 12).

Diseases or pests may still attack even if plants seem to be flourishing and are receiving the best of care.

The best thing to do is to take time during watering to check the leaves (in particular their undersides) and shoots regularly.

How to treat damaged plants

It is important to take measures as soon as problems occur. If you do not, the disease or pest can rapidly spread and even endanger neighbouring plants. Very often, they must then be treated with chemical agents as a last resort.

● Generally, there is nothing one can do about bacterial infections. The best plan is to remove the plants and replace them with new ones.

● Fungal diseases and pests, on the other hand, can usually be controlled quite easily. In the early stages, removal of the infested parts will help. Any cut surfaces should be dusted with charcoal powder to disinfect them. The plants should be destroyed, however, if infestation is severe.

Our tip: Never discard infested plants on your compost heap!

Mechanical control

Mechanical control may help as long as the damage is limited.
● Pests can be removed from the plants by hand or washed off with a vigorous stream of water from a hose.
● Badly infested parts of plants can be cut off.

Biological control

Sticky tags: These are pushed into the soil or compost or are hung on the infested parts of the plants. Pests like white fly or thrips, which are attracted by the colour of the tags, become stuck on the sticky surface.

Pyrethrum-containing agents: These contain an extract of a *Chrysanthemum* species, are effective against aphids, white fly and other sucking insects and are soon broken down again biologically. Unfortunately, they are also harmful to useful insects.

Warning: Agents containing pyrethrum should never be allowed to penetrate an open wound and enter the bloodstream!

Useful insects: The natural enemies of many pests are available through the gardening trade in the form of eggs attached to cards. These are hung on the infested plants. For example, predatory mites can be employed against spider mites and *Cryptolaemus montrouzieri* (Australian ladybirds) against mealy bugs. Their employment does, however, require some patience as they first have to hatch from the eggs or multiply. More recently, useful larvae have also become available in the trade.

You must be careful, however, that you are not simply removing one infestation and replacing it with another!

Non-toxic sprays

● A soap solution is very effective against aphids. Dissolve a little soft soap in water and spray the plants with it.

● Substances containing oil such as paraffin are effective against mealy bugs, scale insects and spider mites. They work by clogging up their respiratory systems.

● Cotton bud sticks soaked in alcohol work the same way in controlling scale insects if the latter are dabbed with the alcohol.

Chemical agents

Chemical plant protection agents should only be employed if all other possible measures have failed. They nearly always tend to be unspecific toxins which means that the insecticides always kill the natural enemies of the pests as well as the pests themselves.

As many of the harmful insects and fungal spores are parasitic and attack only weakened plants, the real cause of the problem is often not treated. In the early stages of infestation it is much more effective to repot the plant, look after it well and remove the pests mechanically or control them by biological means.

The five most frequent diseases

Powdery mildew

Symptoms: a greyish-white layer of fungus on the underside of the leaves; the leaves dry up and fall off. *Cause:* too much humidity together with cool temperatures, not enough circulation of air. *Remedy:* remove any infested leaves.

Downy mildew

Symptoms: a white fungus on the uppersides of the leaves; in severe infestation even on the undersides and the stalks. *Cause:* too warm, humid air. *Remedy:* remove infested leaves. Spray plant with mare's tail extract solution.

Sooty mould

Symptoms: a black, sticky substance, usually on the uppersides of the leaves. *Cause:* sooty mould fungus which settles on the secretions of aphids, scale insects and mealy bugs. *Remedy:* wash off the substance and control the pests.

Verticillium wilt

Symptoms: the leaves at the tips of the shoots wither; the shoot tips turn brown and die off. *Cause:* a fungus which blocks the channels through the vascular tissue of the plant. *Remedy:* difficult, destroy the infested plants and their roots.

Pelargonium wilt

Symptoms: black, decaying stalks, brown to yellowish spots on leaves. *Cause:* bacteria which are spread with infected soil or garden tools. *Remedy:* destroy the plants but do not put them on the compost heap.

It is often also advisable to stand the plants in a different position. Very often the plant will recover by itself. In any case, the pest or disease must be identified properly so that the right agent can be used. The adjoining table will help with your diagnosis.

Handling plant protection agents

● Never use highly toxic substances (marked on the packaging).

● Always follow the manufacturer's instructions for use, dosage and spraying intervals meticulously, to ensure that the substance is used most effectively.

● Always wear rubber gloves when spraying. Never eat, drink or smoke at the same time. Never inhale the spray mist.

● Only ever spray on windless days so that the agent is not dispersed into neighbours' gardens etc.

● Always store plant protection agents in their original packaging, never together with items for human or animal consumption or in a place that is accessible to children or pets.

● Never keep remains of spray or solutions as they will soon lose their effectiveness. Ask your local authority for advice about disposing of them safely.

The five most frequent pests

Red spider mites
Symptoms: fine webs with tiny mites under and between the leaves. White dots on the uppersides of leaves; the leaves dry up. *Cause:* too hot, too dry position. *Remedy:* increase humidity, spray or employ predator bugs.

White fly
Symptoms: green larvae on the undersides of the leaves. White insects. Sticky leaves. *Cause:* overfertilizing with nitrogen-rich fertilizer; air too dry. *Remedy:* increase humidity, use sticky tags and Ichneumon flies.

Aphids
Symptoms: aphids on the undersides of leaves and on young shoots. Crinkled and rolled up leaves; sticky honeydew. *Cause:* a position that is too warm and dry. Overfertilizing with nitrogen. *Remedy:* spray with a soft soap solution.

Mealy bugs
Symptoms: whitish insects and a "woolly" substance covering the stalks and leaf axils. Sticky leaves, malformations. *Cause:* too dry air; lack of nutrients. *Remedy:* use tar oil or an insecticidal spray.

Scale insects
Symptoms: brown, lumpy insects on the leaf ribs and stalks. Sticky honeydew; crippled growth. *Cause:* position too warm and dry; lack of nutrients. *Remedy:* collect the aphids, spray with tar oil.

Index

Numbers in bold indicate illustrations.

Index

Index

Index

Authors' notes

This book describes the arrangement, design and care of hanging and climbing plants on balconies and patios. These plants are primarily grown in large containers. Some of the plants described here are toxic to a greater or lesser degree. Lethally toxic plants or those which are less toxic but which might cause allergies or other health problems, have been marked with a symbol in the tables on pages 10-11 and in the tables accompanying the individual designs (pp. 24, 28, 32, 36 and 40). Please endeavour to make absolutely sure that children and pets do not eat any part of the plants marked as dangerous. Please also make sure that pots, containers, boxes and hanging containers are firmly fixed in safe positions. You will find important notes on this on pages 18, 19, 20 and 21.

It is important to follow the instructions on the packaging of plant protection agents and to observe the recommendations on page 57. Store plant protection agents and fertilizers (including organic ones) where they will be inaccessible to children and pets as their consumption may lead to damage to health. These agents should not be allowed to get into your eyes. If you suffer any minor injuries while handling soil, compost, etc., you should consult your doctor and get professional treatment. Discuss the possibility of having a tetanus vaccination.

Photographic acknowledgements
Becker: pp. 4/5, 22/23, 25 top, 37 top, 44/45, 64/back cover;
Morell: p. 3;
Nickig: inside front cover, pp. 1, 13, 25 bottom, 29 bottom, 33 top, bottom, 43 bottom, 47, back cover top right;
Scherz: pp. 2, 42 bottom, back cover top left;
Schlaback-Becker: p. 54;
Strauss: pp. 15 top, 19, 29 top, 41 top;
Stork: all other photographs.

Plant designs
The arrangements of plants and plant designs on the following pages were specially created for this book by flower arranging artist Martin Weimar: pp. 7, 26/27, 30/31, 34/35, 38/39, 42/43, back cover.

Acknowledgements
The photographer Jürgen Becker and the publishers wish to thank the following garden owners and designers for their kind permission to take photographs:
Boden, Düsseldorf (photo pp. 4/5);
Richard Bödecker (planning), Mettmann (photo p. 22/23);
Bohde, Cologne (photo p. 25);
Trix Botermann, Schoorl, Netherlands (photo p. 37);
Sitje Stuurmann, Bergen, Netherlands (photos p. 4/5 and p. 54).

Cover photographs
Front cover: *Plants on an espalier (design p. 31)*;
Small photo, front cover: *Pandorea;*
Inside front cover: *decorative and mysterious – the flowers of Passiflora caerulea.*
Inside back cover: *The autumnal colours of wild vine and ivy.*
Back cover: left, *climbing rose "Paul's Scarlet Climber"*; right: *Passiflora caerulea;* below: *elegant plants on a patio.*

This edition published 1995 by
Merehurst Limited
Ferry House, 51-57 Lacy Road,
Putney, London SW15 1PR

© 1994 Gräfe und Unzer GmbH, Munich

ISBN 1 85391 438 X

Translated by Astrid Mick
Edited by Lesley Young
Design and typesetting by Cooper Wilson Design
Printed in Singapore by Craft Print Pte Ltd

Beautiful all year round

Some climbing plants are not only lovely in the summer when they produce cheerful, colourful flowers. Certain species, like the wild vine (*Parthenocissus quinquefolia*), produce a regular firework display of colour in the autumn and will drown your patio in a glowing sea of coloured leaves. Other climbing plants also change colour in the autumn. The climbing hortensia (*Hydrangea anomala petiolaris*) is enveloped in shining yellow, while the foliage of grapevines (*Vitis* spp, especially *Vitis vinifera*) changes to burgundy red and golden yellow. Plain evergreen plants, like ivy (*Hedera* spp) or *Euonymus fortunei*, go well with these, as their dark shades of green emphasize the play of autumnal tones.